DISGUSTING ANIMAL DINNERS

Vultures Eat Rotting Corpses!

Miriam Coleman

PowerKiDS press™

New York

Published in 2014 by The Rosen Publishing Group, Inc.
29 East 21st Street, New York, NY 10010

Copyright © 2014 by The Rosen Publishing Group, Inc.

First Edition

Editor: Joanne Randolph
Book Design: Kate Vlachos
Photo Research: Katie Stryker

Photo Credits: Cover Visuals Unlimited, Inc./Dave Watts/Visuals Unlimited/Getty Images; front cover (series title) © iStockphoto.com/lishenjun; back cover graphic -Albachiaraa-/Shutterstock.com; p. 5 chiqui/Shutterstock.com; p. 6 © iStockphoto.com/Giovanni Banfi; p. 7 iStockphoto/Thinkstock; p. 8 Gerrit_de_Vries/Shutterstock.com; p. 9 Ammit Jack/Shutterstock.com; p. 10 dean bertoncelj/Shutterstock.com; p. 11 Jakub Gruchot/Shutterstock.com; pp. 12–13, 18 Pal Teravagimov/Shutterstock.com; pp. 14, 17 claffra/Shutterstock.com; p. 15 (left) artcphotos/Shutterstock.com; p. 15 (right) Sari ONeal/Shutterstock.com; p. 16 Abby Bagnall/Shutterstock.com; p. 19 Jag_cz/Shutterstock.com; pp. 20, 21 Hemera/Thinkstock; p. 22 creativex/Shutterstock.com.

Library of Congress Cataloging-in-Publication Data

Coleman, Miriam, author.
 Vultures eat rotting corpses! / by Miriam Coleman. — First edition.
     pages cm. — (Disgusting animal dinners)
 Includes index.
 ISBN 978-1-4777-2886-4 (library) — ISBN 978-1-4777-2973-1 (pbk.) —
ISBN 978-1-4777-3045-4 (6-pack)
 1. Vultures—Juvenile literature. 2. Vultures—Behavior—Juvenile literature. I. Title.
 QL696.F32C64 2014
 598.9'2—dc23
                              2013024076

Manufactured in the United States of America

CPSIA Compliance Information: Batch #W14PK6: For Further Information contact Rosen Publishing, New York, New York at 1-800-237-9932

CONTENTS

Meet the Vulture

Vultures are nature's **janitors**. They spend their lives cleaning up waste left behind and keeping the outdoors tidy. The waste they clean up just happens to be dead animals, and the way they clean happens to be by eating.

Vultures are carnivores, which means that they eat meat. Almost all other carnivores hunt and kill at least some of the food they eat, but vultures are scavengers. This means that they search out and eat animals that are already dead. Vultures have adapted to be very good at this job. In many places, vultures will find even more to eat than predators that kill for food.

Vultures are large birds. They are around 2 to 3 feet (61–91 cm) tall, with wingspans of 5 feet (1.5 m) or more, depending on the species.

Old World and New World

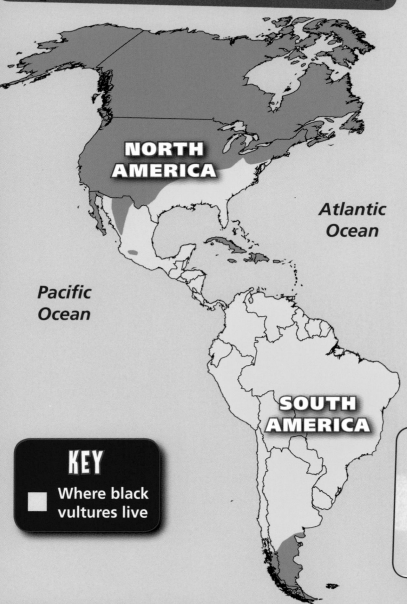

NORTH
AMERICA

Atlantic
Ocean

Pacific
Ocean

SOUTH
AMERICA

KEY

☐ Where black
vultures live

There are 22 **species** of birds called vultures. Although they look very similar and have similar habits, not all of the species are related. The seven vulture species that live in America include the rare California and Andean condors, as well as the common turkey vulture and the black vulture.

There are many kinds of vultures around the world. This map shows the range of the black vulture, which is common in the eastern United States, Central America, and South America.

Here a vulture sits atop an acacia tree in the African savanna.

The American vultures are all related to each other, but they are in a different family from the vultures that live elsewhere in the world. The American species are known as New World vultures and are related to storks. The species that live everywhere else are called Old World vultures and are related to eagles.

Where Do Vultures Live?

Vultures live in North America, Africa, Europe, and Asia. There are no vultures in Australia.

New World vultures live in North, Central, and South America, in forests, deserts, and plains. Some species, such as the turkey vulture, can be found all the way north into Canada and south to Tierra del Fuego and the Falkland Islands, close to Antarctica.

The lappet-faced vulture makes its home in dry places in Africa. It is a huge vulture, with a body that is nearly 4 feet (1 m) tall and a wingspan of up to 9.5 feet (2.9 m)!

King vultures are striking birds with colorful heads and white and black feathers. They look for food in forests and savannas from Mexico to Argentina.

Old World vultures live all over Africa, in the warmer parts of Europe, and in the drier parts of Asia. They are most common in the mountains, deserts, and in the open country.

Vulture Diets

Vultures eat mostly carrion, which is the flesh of dead animals. They might sometimes find fresh meat from animals that have recently died, but often the bodies are **decaying**. Depending on where they live, dinner might be cows and sheep, horses, people, or even dolphins.

Vultures eat as much as they can at every meal because they are never sure when the next one will be. They are able to store some of what they eat in a part called a crop.

Life on the African savanna is hard. Not every animal can survive. These vultures have found a dead zebra on which to feed.

Different species of vultures eat a few other foods as well. Turkey vultures sometimes eat rotten pumpkins, palm fruit, mice, eggs, and animal **feces**. Black vultures also eat garbage and baby birds and turtles. Lappet-faced vultures, which live in Africa, sometimes eat flamingoes. While vultures prefer to eat carrion, they will sometimes hunt and kill live animals if they cannot find enough carrion.

DISGUSTING VULTURE FACTS!

1 If a turkey vulture gets scared, it will often vomit. This might make it lighter so that it can escape predators when it has eaten too much to fly.

2 Bearded vultures eat mostly bones. They swallow small bones whole and drop larger bones onto rocks to smash them into smaller pieces.

3 The king vulture has such a strong bill that it can rip through the armor of an armadillo.

4 Lappet-faced vultures can store more than 13 pounds (6 kg) of food inside themselves at a time.

5 Vultures often pee right on their own legs. This helps keep them cool on hot days. It also cleans off the bacteria from the rotting meat they've been standing in.

6 Vultures sometimes get so messy when they eat that they have to go to a watering hole afterwards to wash all the blood and guts off their faces.

The Nose Knows

Unlike most other birds, some New World vultures have a keen sense of smell. Scientists have found that the part of the brain that detects smell is especially large in the turkey vulture. This sense helps the birds sniff out rotting meat from the air when it can't see the ground through the branches of trees.

Turkey vultures have the best sense of smell of any vulture. They are called turkey vultures because their red heads and black bodies make them look a bit like wild turkeys.

Old World vultures live mostly in open areas, where they can spot their meals from the air. Both Old and New World vultures also depend on their very keen eyesight to find carrion.

Left: This close-up of a turkey vulture's head let's us see its well-defined nostrils. They are excellent at sniffing out rotting meat! *Below*: Vultures soar in the air, often in large groups, looking for food. Black vultures often soar above turkey vultures and count on those birds' keener sense of smell to lead them to food.

Made for Scavenging

Decaying animal corpses are full of bacteria, **parasites**, and other gross things. Vultures have **evolved** so that they have ways to stay safe and clean while getting the most out of carrion. Most vultures' heads are mostly bald, and their neck, feet, and legs have few feathers. This is because they spend a lot of time standing on corpses and sticking their heads inside them.

Here you can see the long neck and curved, sharp beak on this vulture. Notice that there are few feathers on the head and neck. This helps keep vultures clean.

Despite their gross eating habits, vultures work hard to stay clean. They head to take a bath if they get too messy while eating.

That can get pretty messy, and bald skin is easier to keep clean than feathers.

Vultures have long necks that allow them to reach deep inside carcasses to get at the meat. They also have powerful, hooked beaks that they use to tear into flesh.

Acid Insides!

With all the rotting meat and other gross stuff they eat, you might think that vultures would get sick to their stomachs. In fact, vultures can eat food that is dangerous to most other animals. This is because a vulture's stomach acid is so powerful and **corrosive**. It kills the harmful bacteria and parasites that would otherwise make the vulture sick.

Vultures can eat leftovers from other animals' meals that have been lying around in the hot sun for days.

Vultures use their sharp beaks to rip off chunks of meat.

This is helpful to vultures because it means that they don't have to fight other animals for food. No other animals will touch what they can eat. It is helpful to the vultures' **ecosystem** because it prevents the harmful bacteria from spreading.

Vulture Life Cycle

Vultures often live together. Here, a community of vultures is roosting on a rocky outcropping where they have laid their eggs.

Depending on the species, vultures may start breeding when they are between 1 and 10 years old. Most vultures breed just once a year. Old World vultures build nests out of sticks, grass, or carrion fur. New World vultures lay their eggs in shallow holes or in hollow tree stumps.

Most vultures lay just one egg once a year, but some species lay up to three. The parents take turns **incubating** the eggs and searching for food.

Eggs hatch between one and two months later. The parents feed the chicks by **regurgitating** food for them. Young vultures take their first flight after one to six months in the nest. Andean condors can live for over 50 years.

A female vulture sits on her nest with her egg on her feet. Both male and female vultures spend time caring for the eggs and chicks.

A Part to Play

People once feared vultures because of the gross way they dine. We now know, however, that vultures and their disgusting dinners play an important role in the ecosystem. If dead animals are left to lie around, they will soon spread disease and pests. Vultures clean up and make sure that this doesn't happen.

Vultures face many threats, including from farmers who shoot and poison them, cars that run over them, and a scarcity of dead animals to eat. The California condor was once nearly **extinct**. Many countries, including the United States, now have laws to protect the helpful and valuable birds called vultures.

Vultures are often not respected animals. People have a hard time understanding their disgusting diets. However, we should understand that vultures are an important part of our ecosystems.

GLOSSARY

corrosive (kuh-ROH-siv) Having the power to destroy or eat away at something.

decaying (dih-KAY-ing) Rotting.

ecosystem (EE-koh-sis-tem) A community of living things and the surroundings in which they live.

evolved (ih-VOLVD) Changed over many years.

extinct (ik-STINGKT) No longer existing.

feces (FEE-seez) The solid waste of animals.

incubating (IN-kyoo-bayt-ing) Keeping eggs warm, usually at body temperature.

janitors (JA-nuh-turz) People employed as caretakers or cleaners of buildings.

parasites (PER-uh-syts) Living things that live in, on, or with other living things.

regurgitating (ree-GUR-juh-tayt-ing) Throwing up partly eaten food.

species (SPEE-sheez) A single kind of living thing. All people are one species.

INDEX

WEBSITES

Due to the changing nature of Internet links, PowerKids Press has developed an online list of websites related to the subject of this book. This site is updated regularly. Please use this link to access the list: www.powerkidslinks.com/dad/vultur/